This series is a valuable and unique addition to any teacher's resource collection. Each book focuses on a specific character trait - perfectly aligned with the IBO PYP Learner Profile attributes but equally useful for character education in any school with any curriculum. The stories and their characters are very accessible for independent reading, paired / guided reading, and as teacher readalouds. The delightful illustrations further enhance the key ideas and provide lots of detail for students to discover as they browse. The individual style of this series reflects the character of their authors and will be very appealing to teachers and students alike.

Dr. Lesley F. Snowball (CertEd, DipEd, MPhil, PhD) *has been an educator for 35 years, was co-author of the original PYP framework and has published extensively, both independently and for Pearson Education. She is currently Director of Putting it into Practice, providing training and materials support to schools worldwide.*

To thrive in a constantly changing world, today's students need to develop the mindset and skills to become tomorrow's changemakers. ED-ucation Publishing's books will give them a great start.

Charles Tsai, *Founder of Social Creatives, Director of Learning networks for Ashoka Canada, former reporter and producer for CNN, writes and reports on social innovation for Huffington Post*

This book teaches an important lesson that extends far beyond eating meat or vegetables. The characters in the book develop empathy by walking in each other's shoes, teaching young people that to understand themselves, they first need to understand others.

Laurence Levine, *Co-Founder and Director of Kids Can Make a Difference (KIDS)*

The authors have created a story that opens up and deals with the very real issues of food prejudice in today's society as well as the disturbing food culture that has been inflicted on our youth. The taboo of discussing "strange" cultural and the -now more than ever- different world of dietary issues, both personal and medicinal, is addressed in a casual, fun and inspiring story involving two friends. This book will provide a much-needed influence on our children's right and ability to become active in creating good nutritional food for their genre.

Jennifer Schell, *food & wine writer/ columnist and Author of The Butcher, The Baker, The Wine & Cheese Maker - An Okanagan Cookbook*

I really appreciate the message of this book and believe it will open students' minds to the choices we make and why we make them. Unfortunately, our inquisitiveness is often suppressed as we grow to understand societal norms and coolness. This book engages the natural dynamic of curiosity and it could build genuine sensitivity while leading students toward action. Most children understand what vegetarianism is, yet rarely delve into the question of why we eat what we eat, and how this could impact our community and the world around us. This book challenges its readers in a positive way and will help spark some interesting classroom discussions.

Adam Chimienti, *writer for CounterPunch, activist, doctoral candidate, IB educator*

This book presents the cultural, environmental and health issues relating to meat consumption and vegetarianism in a format accessible to children. Rather than watering down these complex issues, we see the characters struggle with understanding each other's perspectives and working through their differences together. While the characters reach a tidy resolution at the book's conclusion, it is through innovation, effort, and teamwork that they create change in their world -- exactly the model we should be putting forth for the next generation of social influencers.

Diana K. Rice, *children's nutrition educator and registered dietitian at Meatless Monday*

It was a regular Tuesday at school.

Mark and Sarah were in line for lunch.

There were only a few options,
so Mark was thinking of getting a burger,
and Sarah was thinking of fries.

"Hey Sarah what's the matter with you,
how come you're not getting a burger?" asked Mark.

"Burgers are gross, and made from cows, or pigs,
or chickens, or lambs - that's why!" said Sarah crossly.

"No, you're gross! There is nothing wrong with a big juicy burger!!
You are always so high and mighty with your ideas!"
shouted Mark.

"You're so close-minded!" Sarah grumbled,
"You don't even know what goes into your big mouth
and the impact it has on the Earth!"

Mark didn't understand Sarah at all,
"Who cares where our food comes from, or the impact it has?
It tastes good, and that's all that matters! Anyway, Sarah,
I am only a kid, what can I do about it?" he asked.

"Forget it, forget I said anything. I don't need a heartless friend like you.
I will just find compassionate people like me to hang out with!!"
fumed Sarah.

"Good idea! I don't even know why I talk to you!
I want to hang out with strong people, not weaklings-
see you later rabbit!" Mark stormed away angrily.

That night Sarah went home and felt really bad about her fight with Mark. It seemed so silly! But she really didn't like that he didn't respect her choice not to eat meat. Still, maybe he was right, maybe she was too high and mighty with her ideas. She thought about ways to end their fight and fix their friendship.

At his own home, Mark was feeling no better. He really liked Sarah! And they had a terrible fight, over food!! He wondered if she had a point. Perhaps he didn't know enough about the food he ate. He thought about some ways he could make up with Sarah.

Mark got on his computer and started to do some research on how his food was made.

He found out that it really did matter what he ate and that even eating a burger had a big environmental impact!

Meanwhile, Sarah was thinking about how meat was a big part of so many cultural celebrations around the world. Sarah thought about how holidays brought her own family together, how she liked it when her relatives got together to laugh, have fun and eat.

She started to understand why people associated meat with happiness and considered how it must make them uncomfortable to think about changing their diets.

Mark's research led him to find information about other cultures. He found out that Hindus don't eat beef because cows are sacred to them. That meant that Mark's burger was really offensive to some people! He found out many athletes and sports-stars are vegetarians or vegans, and that you don't have to live off carrots and lettuce to be vegetarian.

Now he felt bad about calling Sarah a rabbit!

Sarah thought about the times when she had travelled to places and how there were people who had little or no food. Often, even though they had very little, they would still offer her some food to show kindness.

She considered the possibility of travelling to a country where they only had meat to offer, and what would happen if she turned them down. Would that be kind? Perhaps she needed compassion for all the animals of the world, including humans.

Mark was getting excited! He found a lot of yummy alternatives to meat. He found delicious, simple recipes for hearty, healthy meals. He started to think of how he could use some of the meals in his own choices each week. Maybe, he could make each Monday 'meat free'. This would help his impact on the world and he would be making healthy, knowledgeable choices about what he put in his mouth!

Sarah was still thinking about taking care of humans. She was a human, but she didn't take care of herself very well. French fries and potato chips weren't healthy choices, even if they were vegetarian. She wasn't being responsible and making good choices. She didn't feel so high and mighty anymore. She thought about ways she could take better care of herself and what meals were easy and healthy to prepare.

The next day at school, Sarah and Mark saw each other in the hallway.

"I am really sorry that I said you were heartless, Mark" said Sarah, "It wasn't kind of me, and now I understand that it's hard to change your mind about something when it is part of your culture, and family."

Mark felt bad, "I'm sorry too. I shouldn't have said that you were high and mighty. Now I know that my food choices really do impact the whole Earth and I should be more thoughtful about them."

Sarah and Mark walked together to the lunchroom.

But when they got there, what did they see?
Fries and burgers, again!
Sarah and Mark were angry!

But this time instead of being angry at each other,
they got angry at the situation.

Sarah said, "You know, Mark,
we could make a difference, even if we are kids!"

"Yes, we could use all those great recipes I found online and ask the principal to be open-minded to yummy, healthy options for lunch. And maybe we could even do a Meatless Monday!" said Mark excitedly.

"Great idea!" shouted Sarah.

Sarah and Mark went home and worked on a menu plan together.

They presented their idea to the principal
who was impressed with their action.

She asked Mark and Sarah to help teach the chefs some of their recipes
and to teach the other students about what they had learned.

Sarah and Mark were happy.
By being open-minded to each other's ideas
they were able to turn an argument
into a really cool action project that helped their friendship,
their school community and even the Earth!

Did you know this story is a little bit true!
The authors of this book are friends too!

Tosca Killoran is a teacher and has been a vegetarian since 1998! She likes it
when kids are open-minded to other people's perspectives.
Jeff Hoffart is a teacher and a meat eater. He likes kids to discover things that
are important to them and take action!

Learn more about where your food comes from at *petakids.com*

Learn more about Meatless Monday at *meatlessmonday.com*

Did you know there are 10 books in this series? These books all focus on the attitudes and aptitudes found in character education.

Take a peek at the other titles below and get the set here: *www.ED-ucation.ca*

This work has been developed independently from and is not endorsed by the International Baccalaureate (IB)

CPSIA information can be obtained
at www.ICGtesting.com
Printed in the USA
LVIC06n1112010616
490760LV00004B/26